PEEKING PRAIRIE DOGS

by Christine Zuchora-Walske

Pull Ahead Books

Lerner Publications Company • Minneapolis

Website address: www.lernerbooks.com

Curriculum Development Director: Nancy M. Campbell

Words in *italic type* are explained in a glossary on page 30.

Library of Congress Cataloging-in-Publication Data

Zuchora-Walske, Christine.
        Peeking prairie dogs / Christine Zuchora-Walske.
            p.   cm. — (Pull ahead books)
        Includes index.
        Summary: Introduces the physical characteristics, behavior, and habitat of the black-tailed prairie dog.
            ISBN 0-8225-3616-1 (hc. : alk. paper). —
        ISBN 0-8225-3622-6 (pbk. : alk. paper)
            1. Cynomys ludovicianus—Juvenile literature.
        [1. Black-tailed prairie dog. 2. Prairie dogs.] I. Title.
        II. Series.
        QL737.R68Z835   1999
        599.36'7—dc21   98–28517

Manufactured in the United States of America
1 2 3 4 5 6 – JR – 04 03 02 01 00 99

Look! An animal is peeking
out of a hole in the ground.

Can you guess what kind
of animal it is?

This animal is a prairie dog.

It is not really a dog.
It is more like a squirrel.

A prairie dog has a fat, furry body and a short tail.

Prairie dogs eat grass
and other plants.

They pick and eat the plants
with their sharp claws and teeth.

Prairie dogs also use their claws
and teeth to dig *burrows.*

Burrows are
underground
tunnels.
Prairie dogs
live in
burrows.

As a prairie dog digs, it throws dirt out of its burrow.

What will it do with all this dirt?

The prairie dog makes a round
hill of dirt called a *mound.*

The mound makes a ring
around the burrow hole.

The mound helps keep rain from flooding the burrow.

What else is a mound good for?

A prairie dog can sit on a mound and watch for *predators.*

Predators are animals that hunt and eat other animals.

A badger is sneaking near.
Badgers eat prairie dogs.

CHIRK! A prairie dog barks
when it sees a predator.

Other prairie dogs listen
and look around.

If a predator comes too near,
prairie dogs rush underground.

They wait and listen.

The prairie dogs hear
the predator go away.

They peek to make sure
the predator is gone.

YIP!
It is safe
to come
out now!

When prairie dogs bark messages about predators,

they help their families stay safe.

A prairie dog family
is called a *coterie*.

A coterie lives together
in one or more burrows.

Prairie dogs in a coterie
do many things to stay close.

They kiss.

They *groom* each other to
keep their fur clean and neat.

They play together.

They rest together, too.

How does your family stay close?

Baby prairie dogs called *pups*
are born underground in the spring.

Six weeks later, they come
outside for the first time.

Pups stay near their mother.

She teaches them how to find
food and stay safe as they grow.

Pups *nurse* as they grow.

Nursing is drinking milk
from the mother's body.

By fall, the pups are grown-up.
They can dig, bark, and peek.

They can help their coterie
in many ways.

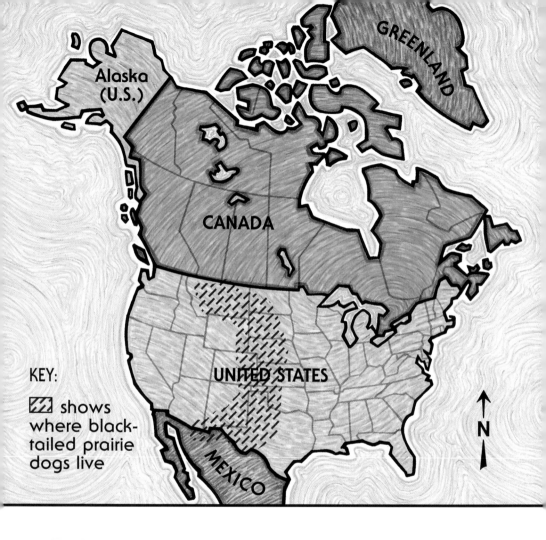

KEY:

▨ shows where black-tailed prairie dogs live

N

Find your state or province on this map.
Do prairie dogs live near you?

Parts of a Prairie Dog's Body

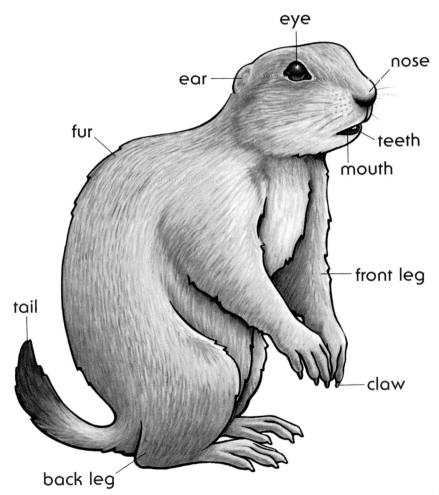

eye

nose

ear

fur

teeth

mouth

front leg

tail

claw

back leg

Glossary

burrows: underground tunnels where some animals live

coterie: a prairie dog family

groom: keep fur clean and neat

mound: a round hill of dirt that makes a ring around a prairie dog burrow hole

nurse: drink mother's milk

predators: animals that hunt and eat other animals

pups: baby prairie dogs

Hunt and Find

- prairie dogs **barking** on pages 14, 17–18
- prairie dogs **digging** on pages 8–10, 27
- prairie dogs **kissing** on page 20
- a prairie dog pup **nursing** on page 26
- prairie dogs **peeking** on pages 3–4, 16
- prairie dogs **playing** on page 22

The publisher wishes to extend special thanks to our **series consultant,** Sharyn Fenwick. An elementary math-science specialist, Mrs. Fenwick was the recipient of the National Science Teachers Association 1991 Distinguished Teaching Award. In 1992, representing the state of Minnesota at the elementary level, she received the Presidential Award for Excellence in Math and Science Teaching.

Ron Zuchora-Walske

About the Author

Christine Zuchora-Walske grew up in Minnesota. She met her first wild prairie dogs when she was a kid, on a family trip to South Dakota's Black Hills. She has liked prairie dogs and traveling ever since then. Christine enjoys doing anything out-doors. She also enjoys reading, making music, and editing books for children. Christine lives in Minneapolis with her husband, Ron.

Photo Acknowledgments

The photographs in this book are reproduced through the courtesy of: © Kent and Donna Dannen, page 10; © Beth Davidow, pages 9, 13, 19, 21; © Jeff Foott, front cover, pages 4, 8, 26, 27, 31; © Rich Kirchner, pages 6, 7, 20, 22; © William Muñoz, page 11; © Frank Staub, pages 3, 12, 14, 15, 17, 18, 23, 24, 25, back cover; © Tom J. Ulrich, pages 5, 16.